SECRET SIN

Praises For *Secret Sin*

Rich Baermann opens up the window to his soul and allows the reader to experience an honest struggle that engaged him for years. His openness and willingness to share his journey will be helpful to many and could be a catalyst to beginning a discussion that, for many, needs to take place.

Dave Wager, President
Silver Birch Ranch
White Lake, WI

I have been privileged to be Rich's brother-in-law for many years. I have witnessed his growth in Christ and his humble walk with the Lord. This book is just an extension of his following, serving and loving His Lord. It is heart-felt and brutally honest and will be a godly challenge to all who read it.

Bill Hoving
Church Planter & Missionary
Baptist Bible Fellowship Int.

In *Secret Sin,* Rich identifies a familiar struggle to many. His vulnerability allows readers to identify, but his work goes far beyond building a bridge of shared experience. Rich articulates the Power that is available to gain victory over sin—any sin. Especially helpful is Rich's parsing of trusting vs. believing and repentance vs. confession.

Steve Sanford, D.Min.
President/Academic Dean
Nicolet Bible Institute

SECRET SIN

A story of one man's sin...

and God's extraordinary love.

Rich Baermann
Forward by Pastor Tim Rezac

Grace Acres Press
Larkspur, CO

Grace Acres Press
P.O. Box 22
Larkspur, CO 80118
(303) 681-9995
www.GraceAcresPress.com

Copyright 2014 Grace Acres Press. All rights reserved.

No part of this publication may be reproduced, stored in a retrieval system, or transmitted in any form or by any means, electronic, mechanical, photocopying, recording, scanning, or otherwise, except as permitted by law, without the prior written permission of the Publisher.

Grace Acres Press also publishes books in a variety of electronic formats. Some content that appears in print may not be available in electronic books.

Library of Congress Cataloging-in-Publication Data:
See GraceAcresPress.com

16 15 14 13   01 02 03 04 05 06 07 08 09 10

All quotations from The Bible obtained through *biblegateway.com* 2010 2011 2012 2013

This book is dedicated to my wife, Barb, whose faithfulness to me deserves the highest praise, and my children, who supported me in my goal of writing a book on a subject that is very personal; so personal that it is rarely addressed at all.

Contents

About the Author ix
Acknowledgments xii
Foreword xi
Introduction xiii
Chapter One: It's Natural!?!? 1
Chapter Two: A "Good Kid" 5
Chapter Three: All's Forgiven 9
Chapter Four: Confessions 13
Chapter Five: Reflections on God's Goodness 19
Chapter Six: What's Up Doc? 21
Chapter Seven: Repentance… or Consequences 25
Chapter Eight: What Do You Call "It"? 31
Chapter Nine: Whom Do You Trust? 37
Chapter Ten: Collateral Damage 45
Chapter Eleven: Choices 49
Chapter Twelve: Blessings in Disguise 53
Chapter Thirteen: To God Be the Glory 59
Conclusion: 63

Foreword

COURAGEOUS SELF-DISCLOSURE

That phrase is how I characterize what you are about to read. This is not inappropriate or prurient self-disclosure, nor is it voyeuristic fluff. I know the author, Rich Baermann, well enough to be convinced of that. Because his natural temperament leans toward introverted and private, the telling of Rich's story was obviously instigated by God. Rich's goal is to help men (and women) develop and maintain healthy habits of sexual purity.

Recently Rich has been ill—*very* ill—with an incurable disease. That disease, it appears to me, has emboldened him to humbly reveal his lifelong struggle with sexual mismanagement to his family, his friends, and now you, the reader. His back and forth battle is a personal description of an all-to-common habit—one that is rarely talked about, especially among the people in the average church. This must, and can, change. Perhaps this book will be a catalyst for that change.

Within these pages you will walk through the frustrating repetitive cycle of confession/progress/failure. Much of Rich's experience is reflective of the sin-cycle of the Apostle Paul as described in Romans 7:14-25—"I do not understand what I do. For what I want to do I do not do, but what I hate I do." As in Paul's quite personal sin-cycle account, I appreciate the theological and life-application balance of Rich's story.

Here is a personal ministry experience that might illustrate one issue cited in this book. Many years ago, in a previous church, I initiated a small group for men called, "Men of Purity." About a dozen men, including me, met together to challenge each other to maintain God-honoring, wholesome sexual purity in the midst of this sex-saturated society. Good news! With caring, mutual accountability, God was healing and strengthening those men. But, a few months into it, we noticed that a few guys started missing meetings. Upon questioning, they said they had to cease attending because of their wives. Rather stunned by that, I asked, "What? I would think your wives would appreciate your efforts?" Their wives were embarrassed by the group's label: "Men of Purity." They could not understand why their husband needed a support group for sexual purity. They took it too personally and became emotionally wounded. "I thought my husband was totally absorbed in me, and satisfied with our sexual intimacy." We eventually changed the name of our group to something generic, like, "Saturday Morning Men's Club."

I find it rather dispiriting that the Christian church community is occasionally quite resistant to this type of realistic, honest, self-disclosure. You know, "Those kinds of things just shouldn't be talked about here". I beg to differ. There are nearly thirty "one another" directives in the New Testament. The church is a community that must be boldly sharing life together ("one another") in all of its successes… and *struggles*. May this book open the window on those kinds of sharing relationships, and may the Spirit of God blow through that window and grip us by His grace, forgiveness, and awesome power. But, it takes audacious candor. It takes a realistic view of sin and self. It takes a long, hard look at 2 Corinthians 7:1—"Dear friends, let us purify ourselves from everything that contaminates body and spirit, perfecting holiness out of reverence for God."

I pray that *Secret Sin* touches many lives with that healing, courageous self-disclosure.

Pastor Tim Rezac
Harvest Bible Chapel
Turks & Caicos Islands

Preface

About the Author

This book was written by an ordinary guy. No claim to fame and no degrees to add importance to what has been written here. This is his first book and, apart from a miracle of God, will probably be his last for reasons that will become clear once you begin reading it. He is just someone trying to be honest about his failings and feelings and hoping to pass on what he has learned in the process of living life to his family and to you.

You probably won't see his name on any "Who's Who" list, because apart from the notoriety attained by this book, Rich hasn't done anything exceptional So it is with great anticipation his that he has finally offered his true story to the world in hopes that by doing so God's truth may be revealed to you. Rich knows that his story has remained a secret for far too long.

Rich was an employee of Electro-Motive Diesel, formerly Electro-Motive Division of General Motors, for thirty-two years before an illness prevented him from continuing. He began his career there as an electrical inspector and progressed to a Sequencer, providing the "where" and "when" of manufacturing locomotives. He also spent twenty-five of those years attending and serving at

Emmanuel Baptist Church, Berwyn, IL (later Emmanuel Bible Church) where much of his education regarding the Scripture took place under Pastor Richard E. Wager. Rich hopes that by sharing his struggle with the world he might be able to help others understand their struggles and Christ's love more fully.

Acknowledgements

I am extremely grateful that we have a God of second (and many more) chances who can redeem the sorriest of circumstances that we have created through our disobedience of Him and glorify Himself while forgiving and blessing us in the process.

I am thankful to the publisher and friend Anne Fenske for her help and caring expertise in every aspect of bringing my story to print.

I am grateful to V for the professional evaluation of the book and the impact that it had on me and the book's message.

I appreciate and want to offer special thanks to my eloquent friend Pastor Tim Rezac for offering his special touch to the book's Foreword.

I want to thank all of the friends who read the book and valued it enough to offer their endorsements.

Introduction

Life. The Bible says that each man's life is but a breath (Psalm 39:5, NIV). That truth is usually the farthest thing from our minds, especially when we're young. We may live each day of our lives without a thought about death, until one day we find ourselves looking back on the years that have passed and asking if they turned out to be all that we once hoped that they would be. Did our dreams become realities, were they unfulfilled, or did we fail to dream at all? What did we accomplish? What do we regret? Inevitably, it's the regrets that usually leap to the forefront of our thoughts. We may find ourselves thinking about the mistakes we made; what we wish we had or hadn't done. We may think about the actions that have shaped our lives and wonder if, or how, our lives might be different now if we had chosen another path in the past. It's then that the "if only's" start to consume our thoughts and we may begin to despair. If only I had done this; if only I hadn't done that. We may wonder whether all is lost. We may wonder whether there is time left to right our sinking ship. We may wonder whether some good can result from what appears to be the result of our own poor choices.

This is the place where I have been. These are the thoughts that have both raced through my mind and weighed heavily on my heart as I dealt with the reality of being diagnosed with a disease for which there is no cure. What caused it? Did my poor choices cause it? Did God cause it? Is God angry with me? Is He punishing me? Can there be any hope that He still cares about me? Will He rescue me from my presumed sure fate? I have sought answers to all of these questions and have found what I believe to be clear answers to some while others remain unclear. What is clear to me is that God has a purpose for everything, and His purposes are always good because He is good.

My daughter gave me a gift for my sixty-fourth birthday. It was Billy Graham's book *Nearing Home*. He concludes chapter one with these words, "What testimony are you passing on to others following you? Remembering what God has done for you will invigorate you in old age. Others are watching your actions and attitudes. Don't diminish the impact you can make; pass on foundational truths of God's Word... (Thomas Nelson Inc., 2011)." So it is in that spirit that I share this part of my journey through life with you; hoping that if you find yourself in the place in life where I have been, you might find hope in Him, and be invigorated as you discover God's will and unique purpose for your life. If you are young and just beginning the journey, you might consider carefully the patterns of life that you are establishing and will make the changes that will allow you to live a richer and fuller life that is free from regret.

You may not agree with all that I will say here. You may not agree with my stance on the main subject of discussion and some of the conclusions that I reach, but I will do my best to help you understand how I came to my beliefs. I know that even if you don't agree, you will defend my right to make the statements that I have made and I hope that you will, at the very least, accept my conclusions as God's instruction for my life. However, if you do agree, my hope is that at least some of my conclusions become your convictions, and that you glorify God by following them for all of the remaining days of your life.

My plan is to start each chapter by telling you a portion of my story to be followed by a "So What About…?" section that I've added to offer some explanation, if needed, about the conclusions that I've drawn. I'll also attempt to anticipate some of the questions that you may have for me along the way. I'll end the chapter by giving you one or two verses to consider that will reinforce what I have said. I hope that format will keep me on track and will be profitable for you as well. All that I would ask of you is that you reserve judgment on the conclusions that I reach until I can explain them more fully later in the chapter and that you'd remember that, right or wrong, those were actually my thoughts and feelings at the moment.

It's Natural!?!?

WHAT WAS IT that caused me to be in this place? What were these poor choices that I made? For me, the answer is the choice to follow the desires of my sinful nature and the habit and resulting addiction that was born out of that choice. It's about a life affected by the practice of masturbation (there, I've said it).

I don't know what your views on this subject are, but I'm fairly certain that the vast majority of readers are personally acquainted with this practice (if they are "normal"—according to those who have researched the subject). I'm also fairly certain that it hasn't come up in any conversation recently, except maybe jokingly. I'm fairly certain because WebMD.com answers the question *"Who Masturbates?"* by stating that they have found the answer to that question is:

> "Just about everybody. Masturbation is a very common behavior, even among people who have sexual relations with a partner. In one national study, 95% of males and 89% of females reported that they have masturbated. Masturbation is the first sexual act experienced by most males and females. In young children, masturbation is a normal part of the growing child's exploration of his or her body. Most people continue to masturbate in adulthood, and many do so throughout their lives."

Add the fact that it is number two on the list of Bible.com's top 20 questions "*What does The Bible say about...*" right after homosexuality, and I'm led to believe that most people are doing it, almost nobody is talking about it, and many people are curious or feeling guilty about it.

Let's start by letting WebMD.com define it for us. The website says that "Masturbation is the self-stimulation of the genitals to achieve sexual arousal and pleasure, usually to the point of orgasm (sexual climax)." In answering the question "*Is Masturbation Normal?*" it states:

> "While it once was regarded as a perversion and a sign of a mental problem, masturbation is now regarded as a normal, healthy sexual activity that is pleasant, fulfilling, acceptable and safe. It is a good way to experience sexual pleasure and can be done throughout life."

It goes on to say that,

> "Masturbation is only a problem when it inhibits sexual activity with a partner, is done in public, or causes significant distress to the person."

And then it warns that,

> "It may cause distress if it is done compulsively and/or interferes with daily life and activities."

In addition, in answer to the question, "*Is Masturbation Harmful?*" WebMD.com states:

> "In general, the medical community considers masturbation to be a natural and harmless expression of sexuality for both men and women. It does not cause any physical injury or harm to the body, and can be performed in moderation throughout a person's lifetime as a part of normal sexual behavior. Some cultures and religions oppose the use of masturbation or even label it as sinful. This can lead to guilt or shame about the behavior."

It further states:

> "Some experts suggest that masturbation can actually improve sexual health and relationships. By exploring your own body through masturbation, you can determine what is erotically pleasing to you and can share this with your partner. Some partners use mutual masturbation to discover techniques for a more satisfying sexual relationship and to add to their mutual intimacy"

So, if you've had any questions about it, you should be feeling side pretty good about those answers.

Now, let's hear the other side of the debate from Bible.com.

"God cares about what we do with our bodies, in public or in private. He doesn't want us to abuse ourselves in any way. In fact, an older definition of masturbation is 'self-abuse'. Although more modern dictionaries may no longer carry this definition, they are still linked together under self-abuse:

Self-abuse noun
 1. Abuse of oneself or one's abilities
 2. Masturbation"

Bible.com continues by saying:

"First of all, masturbation will not truly relieve the sexual pressure that one may feel. It may for a short moment, but in the long run it only creates a deeper desire and capacity for sex, which will lead to more masturbation. If you let yourself become enslaved to a sexual high, you will find that you need to go to increasingly extreme acts to maintain the same degree of excitement. There are even ungodly sex therapists who recommend masturbation as a way of increasing sexual desire, not lessening it. This creates a vicious circle, like the junkie who craves a 'fix', but is only temporarily satisfied. The more he indulges in his dependency, the more ensnared by addiction he becomes."

Finally, from the website treatment-centers.net in an article entitled *"Sexual Addiction and Sex Addiction Recovery"* we find this statement.

"*Sex addiction* can involve a wide variety of practices. A large number of sex addicts say their unhealthy use of sex was a progressive process. It may have started with an addiction to masturbation, pornography (either printed or electronic), a relationship, multiple relationships, or a series of one-night-stands, but over the years progressed to increasingly dangerous behaviors."

So What About…?

First of all, you may be asking why I chose to quote these particular websites. Let me assure you that a sinister plot was not involved here. I chose them because they happened to be the first places that I went to look for information about the subject, and frankly, I was surprised by some of what I found. If you were shocked by Bible.com's reference to the definition of "self-abuse", they (in a sense) were reporting what they found. WebMd.com will only report from a scientific point of view while Bible.com comments from a spiritual perspective.

I can't say that I am a complete proponent of what any of these websites have to say about the subject, but with all of the competing voices proposing vastly different outcomes from the practice of masturbation, what do you believe?

Secret Sin \ Baermann

I would suggest that it would be wise to decide. Do you believe that it is a sin; do you believe it's not? Do you believe it could be both? There's a verse below that supports the fact that something could seem right when in it's actually wrong. It just might be that hearing my story will help you decide if you haven't already or may cause you to change your decision if you've already made up your mind.

> **There is a way that appears to be right, but in the end it leads to death.**
> **—Proverbs 14:12, NIV**

A "Good Kid"

I CAN'T RECALL exactly when it started, but my first recollection of masturbation dates back to my preteen years. I probably didn't know that it was called masturbation, and there are several other ways that it's referred to conversationally that are rather crude. So, rather than sounding offensive or having to type the word masturbation hundreds of times, I'll refer to it as "it", now that we know what the "it" is that we're talking about. I'm sure that I started doing "it" just because it felt good.

I was a rather shy child. I began noticing girls, and as I grew older the female form became more interesting and attractive to me. There were certain girls that I had a crush on at school, and I began to have sexual fantasies about them, but I hadn't started dating anyone. My thoughts began to turn towards them when I did "it", or a piece of woman's advertising for lingerie or an occasional men's magazine.

My parents always said that I was a good kid. I rarely got into trouble and almost never required disciplining. My folks were members of a mainstream religious denomination, and I was raised with a sense of morality based on a set of do's and don'ts that included a no sex before marriage policy on dating. I thought I had a clear sense of right and wrong and tried to steer clear of doing anything that would get me into trouble. So when I started dating, during my final years of high school, having sexual intercourse was a line that I just would not cross. That was just wrong according to my way of thinking on the matter.

It was during my second year of college that I met the young lady that would eventually become my wife. I was twenty and Barb was nineteen. As I look back on our dating relationship, I have to confess that I didn't treat her with the respect that she deserved from someone who professed to love her. It wasn't that I crossed the self-imposed line that I had created, but I often went beyond what was appropriate and then I'd do "it". After about six months of dating, I enlisted in the Air Force and, apart from periodic leaves of absence, our relationship continued via phone calls and letters for the next fifteen months. I continued to do "it" during that time of separation and it was during that extended time apart that we became engaged and finally married. We had remained committed to the no sex before marriage policy in accordance with my religious upbringing and were free from the guilt that could have resulted from premarital sexual experiences (or so I thought).

Our honeymoon was spent taking in the sites as we drove across the country back to Travis Air Force Base, Fairfield, CA where I was stationed. Barb was away from home for the first time, having left her family behind to live with this "stranger". Our home was a small, one bedroom apartment located off base, in town. It was almost as though I had a regular job, although I worked the graveyard shift at the base. There were a number of military couples that lived in the same apartment complex. So our transition into married life went well, even aided by the fact that we were two thousand miles from home with only each other to run to when we had a problem.

We had been married for about sixteen months when Barb became pregnant according to plan. She had been using birth control, but we wanted to have our first child while I was still in the service to avoid the costs of the pregnancy. So everything went according to plan and the result was a beautiful baby girl. Seven months later I was honorably discharged after having served for four years, and our little family headed back to Illinois and civilian life.

So What About…?

You might say that since I was a good kid, it was natural for me to want to follow a no sex before marriage policy and that desire actually made masturbation a good way to avoid premarital sex and relieve the sexual pressure that a teenage boy begins to experience. But with that positive came an even more problematic negative in that "it" became a lifetime habit. This was not a good thing, but does not necessarily make it sin, to which I would say, you're right—technically.

In an article called *Grappling with the Definition of Sin* written by Richard Wagner from *Christianity for Dummies,* he defines sin this way:

2 \ A "Good Kid"

> Sin is any deliberate action, attitude, or thought that goes against God. You may think of sin as an obvious act, such as murder, adultery, or theft. Although that's true, sin is also wrongdoing that's far subtler and even unnoticeable at times, such as pride, envy, or even worry. Sin includes both things you shouldn't have done, but did *(sins of commission)* and things you should've done, but didn't *(sins of omission).*

I believe that to be an accurate definition. If it is true, we probably don't acknowledge most of the sin in our lives. A little later in the article he states the fact that "Anything not 100 percent sin-free is impure — 99.99 percent isn't good enough. According to James 2:10, even one itty-bitty sin over the course of a lifetime is too much."

I think that Wagner makes a very important point when he talks about sin. That point is if a thought or action isn't 100% pure it is a sin. When we consider masturbation, I would guess that 99.9% of the time it is accompanied by an impure thought. In my case, I confessed that I had thought about certain girls, women's advertising, or an occasional men's magazine. According to that definition you'd have to say that when I would do "it", I was sinning. My mind certainly wasn't blank at the time. However, that does leave the possibility that you could do "it" without sinning, if you could do "it" without thinking an impure thought.

I know that I shared a quote from WebMd.com in the first chapter that says, "Masturbation is the first sexual act experienced by most males and females. In young children, masturbation is a normal part of the growing child's exploration of his or her body." You may be inclined to say that since children masturbate, it can't possibly be a sin. My response would be that it is evidence of the fact that we are born with a sin nature that is prone to take virtually anything that God has intended for good and pervert it into something evil. It may not be considered a sin when the child first begins to practice it, but "it" may become a sin sometime later when it is coupled with an impure thought. There may be other instances where God doesn't consider masturbation to be a sin, but I would say that as we become older it generally becomes more and more difficult to meet God's standard of purity.

For example, and we've all seen it. Little Johnnie takes his brother's toy away from Him without a question being asked. It's all simply a matter of I see it, I want it, and *I will* take it. No remorse, no regrets. Then Johnnie's mother says "NO, Johnnie! Don't do that! That's bad!", and Johnnie learns, over a period of time, that just taking his brother's toy is wrong. But every once in a while Johnnie wants to play with that toy without asking his brother, because sometimes his brother isn't very nice and says no when Johnnie asks. So Johnnie now has to make a choice between doing what is right and asking (even though he doesn't want to) and doing what his mother has told him is wrong and facing the potential consequences. If he makes the right choice, he may not get what he wants at that moment, but he doesn't have to be worried about what he may have to face later. If he makes the wrong choice, he may get what he wants now and may even escape the consequences of his disobedience for the time being, but he should be concerned about the possibility of future consequences. Choosing sin is *always* the wrong choice, and sin *always* has consequences.

My parents' overall evaluation of me as a good kid was slightly inaccurate when compared to God's assessment: All have turned away, all have become corrupt; there is no one who does good, not even one (Psalm 14:3, NIV). This is so often the case when we are judged according to God's holy standard rather than man's arbitrary laws.

> I was sinful at birth, sinful from the time my mother conceived me.
> —Psalm 51:5, NIV

> For whoever keeps the whole law and yet stumbles at just one point is guilty of breaking all of it.
> —James 2:10, KJV

All's Forgiven

During my years in the military I had stopped attending church regularly, and Barb and I rarely attended as a couple while we were in California. In fact, when our daughter was born we didn't even have her baptized which was a given according to my parents beliefs. It wasn't that we didn't feel the need to include God in our lives. Rather, it was that we had been raised under the teachings of different mainline Protestant faiths, a reality that my parents were not too pleased about, and we still hadn't settled on which one we wanted to adopt as a couple.

It wasn't too long after we returned home to Illinois that Barb's brother talked to us about where we were at spiritually. He had been saved at a Billy Graham crusade, and we had expressed to him our dissatisfaction with our church-going experience since returning. He told us about his experience and even invited us to services at his church. The experience felt somewhat strange to us and caused us to decide that we weren't quite ready to make his newly found faith ours. He suggested that we might find what we were searching for somewhere other than the churches that our parents attended and suggested some alternatives; places where he thought we would be sure to hear the truths of the Bible taught. Soon after, we began attending the Bible Church that was located in a community nearby.

As we regularly attended our new church and heard messages from the Senior Pastor, we began to understand the teachings that we had heard before in a new way. First and foremost was that Jesus didn't come to earth as a baby, live a sinless life, and die on a cross for our sins so that we would have to live a life of trying to be good enough to get to heaven. He came, lived, and died because none of us could be good enough; no matter how hard we tried. He died so that we didn't just have to hope we've been good enough to get there after we die; we could be sure because He was good enough. The only thing that we needed to do is to put all of our faith in what He had already done for us and quit hoping that our goodness would get us there. We learned that each person needs to put their faith in Jesus and trust in His death and resurrection as payment for their sins; that going to heaven after you die isn't the result of being born into a certain family or attending a certain church.

What also became clear to me, as I learned more about what the Bible really said, was that I was a sinner (we all are). I wasn't a fairly good person who hopefully was on his way to heaven; I was a sinner definitely on his way to hell, and it was one particular sin that convinced me. Now, we can debate whether or not my habit ("it") was sinful, but you can't argue with what my conscience was telling me. My conscience had condemned me and the sentence was sure. I needed someone to pardon me and that someone was Jesus. I wasn't going to make it to heaven without Him.

It was during a visit to our home by our pastor that he posed the question to Barb and me, "Have you ever prayed to receive Christ as your personal Savior?" He was asking us if we had told God that we personally believed in what Jesus had done on our behalf and that we wanted to place our trust in Him, rather than our goodness, to get us to heaven. We hadn't done that, but we were both ready to take that step. That night, in our little dining room, Jesus became more to me than the one who died for the sins of the world. He became *my* Savior; the One who died for *my* sins. I was forgiven!

So What About…?

I had just done the most important thing I would ever do, or so I thought. The thing is, what I'd done didn't change me the way that I had expected. Since I was a pretty good guy by the world's standards, I didn't have anything visible to give-up. I didn't smoke, hardly drank, didn't chew (and didn't go with girls who do). I was a model Baptist before I became a Baptist. The only thing that was wrong with me was my little secret and I wasn't telling. The one thing that needed to change didn't. In essence, I wasn't any different than I was before I got saved… or was I?

Well, I certainly didn't look any different, but I was. My life hadn't been changed completely yet outwardly, but Jesus had changed me inwardly.

3 \ All's Forgiven

I would sin again, but as abhorrent as that sin was to God, it had now been and forever would be transferred to Jesus' his account and removed from mine. Every time I would do "it," His mercy and forgiveness would flow like Jesus' blood over me working its wonderful miracle of forgiveness in me. I wish that I wouldn't have disappointed Him by not fully recognizing the reality of that truth sooner and offered Him praise for it. I could have experienced the victory and freedom that I was searching for if I had grasped the truth of 2 Corinthians 5:17: Therefore, if anyone is in Christ, he is a new creation. The old has passed away; behold, the new has come.

> There is therefore now no condemnation for those who are in Christ Jesus.
> —Romans 8:1, ESV

> Because of our faith, Christ has brought us into this place of undeserved privilege where we now stand, and we confidently and joyfully look forward to sharing God's glory.
> —Romans 5:2, NLT

Confessions

It wasn't long after we were saved that Barb gave birth to another beautiful, healthy baby girl. We continued to attend church services regularly and I began to serve at the church by becoming an usher. We grew in our new found faith, but I continued to do "it" occasionally. The habit that had been a part of my life prior to becoming a Christian was not so easily done away with. I continued to supplement physical intimacy with my wife with "it" even though it's what had convinced me that I was a sinner. If you're asking why I would continue to do such a thing, the answer is because "it" was a habit, but it wasn't really hurting anyone (or so I thought).

After several years, and after Barb became pregnant with our third child, we concluded that the little two bedroom home that we had been living in would soon become too small for our family. So we purchased a small three bedroom duplex in an adjoining town, but we continued to attend services at the church where we had been saved. It was shortly after we moved into our new home that our son was born. We were overjoyed to have a boy in the family to carry on the family name, but a few weeks after his birth our joy was replaced by concern. The doctor had found a birth defect that would require surgery to repair. Feeling powerless to do anything else, we sought to gain God's favor by offering this gift that He had given to us back to Him to do with as He pleased in exchange for a favorable outcome. God answered our prayer by using the skilled hands of a heart surgeon to repair the defect in his aorta using a procedure that rarely had been performed on someone so young. All that would be required were periodic check-ups as our son matured. Needless to say, we were eternally thankful for what God had done. It was evident to us that God was good.

It was when our son was approximately two years old that we decided to look for another church. Close friends of ours who had attended our former church had moved out of state. Since we had no other close ties there, we started attending a similar church a bit nearer to our home. Our new church was suggested by Barb's sister and brother-in-law, who had begun attending there. They introduced us to a couple they had met and, because he was a fellow golfer, we became fast friends. My new friend was involved in several ministries at the church, the church choir being one. So I became a member of the choir and made several other new friends. He also served as an elder, and after our relationship grew he eventually asked me if I would consider serving in that capacity as well. I agreed, so he recommended me for election to the Elder Board and I was subsequently approved and elected by the congregation for my first three year term.

I was now thirty-five, an Elder, and part of the top leadership of the church. No one knew of my habit and, although I had tried to rid my life of the practice, it continued to be something I returned to from time to time. It seemed as though I would experience seasons of victory over it, only to fall back into doing "it" again. My desire was to be free from its control, and each time I relapsed I felt the guilt of failure again. I confessed my sin to God, but I had a difficult time accepting the fact that my sin was forgiven because I had confessed doing "it" so many times before. I struggled to cultivate the habit of Bible reading and prayer, and although I dismissed the problem with the excuse that I just lacked the discipline that was required, I wondered if it had something to do with my sin.

In addition to the difficulties in my relationship with God, Barb began expressing her frustration with the state of our relationship. She lamented over our less than frequent physical intimacy and the lack of emotional and spiritual intimacy in our marriage. I was also starting to experience some occurrences of ED, erectile dysfunction. I knew that I needed to confess my secret to her to explain what I believed was the source of the problem, so I eventually mustered the courage to 'fess up. To my surprise she was surprisingly understanding and forgiving of my failure, but demanded that I seek help with my addiction by getting some counseling and see a doctor. I was in full agreement, so I went to a urologist, who gave me a prescription for some little purple pills, and then I visited my pastor for suggestions regarding counseling. He graciously accepted my confession and recommended that I see a professional counselor. For the first time I anticipated real progress in my battle to be free at last.

4 \ Confessions

I began to meet with the gentleman that my pastor had recommended, and after a number of sessions he attempted to convince me that I wasn't really such a bad guy. After all, I had never been unfaithful to my wife, had always provided for my family, and had never committed any crimes or done drugs. Of course, I know I'm over simplifying what he said, but that was the gist of it. Now this may have been a case of selective hearing, but that's what I came away with at the end of my counseling.

Needless to say, the counseling didn't provide the answer that I was seeking. I'm not sure that I would have recognized the answer if it had hit me in the face. I continued to search for someone who would hold me accountable for my actions; who would force me to stop my insanity. I decided that my close friend and fellow elder might be the someone that I was looking for; a guy that cared about me enough to consistently inquire about how I was doing and would confront me regarding my sin. So I confessed "it" to my friend and asked him if he would hold me accountable concerning the practice. He agreed, and my hopes were buoyed again by the prospect of victory.

I continued to serve as an elder and even was elected Chairman of the Elders by my peers after serving a number of terms. I continued to escape into my habit periodically for reasons which weren't remotely clear to me. My friend and I met occasionally for accountability, but he was too nice to inquire or confront me, if necessary, about my problem. I questioned whether or not it was right to continue to remain an elder and decided to confess my sin to my fellow elders and let them determine my fate. I felt that they had a right to know, so I proceeded to inform them of my habit and found them to be accepting rather than condemning. They suggested that I find someone who would hold me to a higher standard of accountability for my life in general, but none of them volunteered for the assignment. They asked if there was someone who might fill that role and one person did come to mind. My choice was acceptable to them, so they told me to contact him and wished me well without the need for further action.

My new accountability partner was also a friend, although not a close one. He had always impressed me as a man who was close to God, so I looked forward to the prospect of spending time with him in the hope that some of his godly habits might rub off on me. I thought that he, of all people, should be an elder, but he felt that he was disqualified because he had been divorced many years earlier. We began to meet regularly, and, of course, the first order of business was another confession on my part. I was beginning to feel as though the whole world knew about my secret sin. As we continued to meet, we talked about many aspects of life, but my habit wasn't the subject of our conversation very often. I guess that "it" was more of an issue to me than to anyone else. To be honest, although our conversations were good, I didn't change as much as I had hoped that I would because of the time that we spent together. I don't even remember how often that I had been practicing my habit during that time. All that I know is that I didn't stop doing "it" as a result of our accountability sessions. As an aside, I should mention that I started to experience some twitching in my leg when I would do "it".

Our times together ended as result of a major relocation. Barb and I decided that we should move fifty miles west of where we were living to be nearer to her folks. Her mom began to have some health issues and we wanted to be closer so that Barb could help care for her, not knowing what the future might hold. So we left our church, and I my elder position, and began a new life. Of course, the move also caused us to look for a new church home, and after several months we landed at a church where a young man that had been on staff at our previous church years earlier was now serving. He was the Youth Pastor, but one of his responsibilities was to oversee a ministry called *Celebrate Recovery*, which ministered to people with habits, hurts, and hang-ups. How much clearer could it have been that this was where God wanted me?

Celebrate Recovery was similar to Alcoholics Anonymous except our higher power had a name; it was God. There was a curriculum provided that we worked through individually and then met once a week to discuss with a small group of individuals (including my friend, the Youth Pastor, who led the group) that stayed together throughout the program. By now it had become easy to talk about my habit, so this confession was a breeze. Besides, these guys all had issues themselves, so it wasn't as though I was the only sick person. We progressed through the steps and I completed the program, but had I really changed? Was the victory that I had sought for so long really mine?

It was shortly thereafter that my friend felt called by God to leave his position at the church and plant a new church in a nearby town. So Barb and I decided to follow him and help with the new venture. Our fledgling church began meeting in a school and there was much work to be done with few workers. This was also the case with regard to leadership. So, knowing that I was a leader at the church where we had first met, my friend who was now the Pastor asked me to become part of a leadership team that he was forming. I agreed. It felt good to be useful again after what seemed like a long time since I had been involved as an elder. And how was I doing concerning my habit, you ask? To tell you the truth, I'm not sure. I do remember that it was becoming less do-able because of my ED problems, and by now intercourse was out of the question. As I said before, there were extended times when I would seemingly experience victory over "it", only to succumb to temptation again. This was one of those periods. I can tell you in retrospect that, although I may not have been involved in my habit at the time, it would still impact my life in a way that I wouldn't have imagined in the years to come.

4 \ Confessions

So What About...?

At one point I use the word addiction to refer to my secret sin. You might question whether or not that is accurate because I describe my involvement as being occasionally, from time to time, and periodically. If we define masturbation addiction as the compulsive need to masturbate, rather than thinking of the frequency as being the deciding factor as to whether or not I meet the qualifications, I think that the fact that I just couldn't stop or didn't want to qualifies me as an addict. Even though I didn't do "it" that frequently at times, I was enslaved to "it". We can ask exactly how often you have to do it to be considered an addict, but I don't think that anyone could offer an exact answer to that question,

In addition, you might say that I have an overly guilty conscience. My response would be to give thanks to God. I'd rather have a conscience that still hears God's voice than one than one that has grown deaf to His correction. Having an overly guilty conscience does not seem to be a disease of epidemic proportions these days. We spend a great deal more time justifying our actions than taking ownership of them. We make provision for sin far too often and strive for purity far too infrequently.

There was a time when I prayed that God would make me less sensitive to sexual stimulus, thinking that would help me find the victory that I was looking for over this sin. He needed to do much more. He needed to give me new heart on the matter. That's why I talk about searching for victory versus accepting change. I needed a new self, not just a slightly improved version of the old self. The fact is I already had it: I just didn't realize it.

One night when I was either having a problem sleeping or a nightmare (I'm not sure which), the thought came to me of a plot that was carried out by Satan to keep people from getting to heaven. Now I know that this couldn't actually happen because God has protected His Word throughout the centuries, but Satan was able to get the "m-word" removed from every existing copy of the Bible as if it never was there. It wasn't long before it was forgotten, and millions of people who never knew it was a sin because it wasn't mentioned ended up in hell as a result.

What if that actually happened? Well, I know that God is just, and that He would make some kind of provision for those who were misled, but the reality is it doesn't matter. Why? We are already forgiven if Christ is our Savior. I know that we are told to confess our sins, but I believe that's more for our benefit than God's. You see, we're all going to commit a multitude of sins throughout our lifetime. We're going to be aware of some, some we won't; we're going to remember some, some we'll forget. It's as though you had Alzheimer's disease and were unaware of what you were doing sometimes and you'd forget what you did at other times. The issue is whether or not we are aware of our sinfulness and our need for Christ's sacrifice. If we confess the sins we are aware of, the rest will be taken care of and we won't have to be concerned about whether we've confessed them all.

> If we claim we have no sin, we are only fooling ourselves and not living in the truth. But if we confess our sins to him, he is faithful and just to forgive us our sins and to cleanse us from *all* wickedness.
> —1 John 1:8-9, NLT, emphasis mine

> When you follow the desires of your sinful nature, your lives will produce these evil results: sexual immorality, impure thoughts, eagerness for lustful pleasure…
> —Galatians 5:19, NLT

Reflections on God's Goodness

LOOKING BACK upon our thirty-eight years of marriage, I am amazed at how good that God had been to Barb and me. So I thought that it would be good to get you caught up on some of the details of my story that I've neglected.

Because of Barb's faithfulness to me, we are still married, and God had blessed us with three children and nine grandchildren. I have never been unemployed, and only had three jobs (the last of which lasted for twenty-nine years). Barb had been able to be a stay-at-home mom until our oldest headed off to college, and worked just part-time after that. Our kids have participated in activities at church and spent a week at a Christian camp each summer throughout their school years. Our oldest finished college, is married, has four children, and lives in Wisconsin where her husband was on staff at the camp they had gone to as kids. Our other daughter is also married to a Christian guy that she knew while growing up. In fact, he is the brother of her closest friend. He is a grade school P.E. teacher and she is caring for their two girls by being a homemaker. Our son finished college, met a young lady while serving at that same Christian camp, and is now married with three kids. He owns his own business and they settled in Chicago to minister to the people of the city.

God has been so gracious to us. We aren't perfect parents by any stretch of the imagination. Of course, we prayed for our kids as they grew up, and made an effort to place them in situations where they would be influenced by Christian people and principles. Although we experienced a few bumps in the road as they grew older, you can see that God was incredibly faithful to us, as evidenced by the outcome of those choices.

God has also been faithful in providing for our needs. Early on in our Christian journey we decided to tithe, which is giving ten percent of our income to the church. We also made the decision that Barb would be a homemaker and would make it her full-time responsibility to be there for the kids and me. God honored that commitment with steady employment for me and the wherewithal to increase our giving to a few other ministries as well. We aren't rich by American standards, but we certainly live well when compared to many in the rest of the world.

In addition to all of the many ways that he cared for us, he also blessed us with good health and shielded us from major illness. He even allowed me to indulge in my hobby of golf by allowing us to purchase a home located in a golf course community.

God demonstrated his love for us by blessing us beyond measure. He also enriched us with the experiences of serving. I neglected to mention the period that I served as Worship Leader at the church where I had been an elder, an opportunity that I never would have imagined, or the weekly Bible study at work. He blessed me richly and was faithful to me in spite of my ongoing sin and unfaithfulness to Him

> He does not treat us as our sins deserve or repay us according to our iniquities.
> —Psalm 103:10, NIV

What's Up Doc?

WE HADN'T BEEN at the new church for more than a year when my mother-in-law's health took a turn for the worse and she went home to be with the Lord. She and Barb were very close, and with the physical loss came loneliness and a sense of lost purpose. Barb began to feel a need to be closer to our kids and grandchildren. So we sold our home and moved an hour and a half north to be nearer to our younger daughter and her family. We built a house and our daughter and son-in-law surprised us by deciding to build down the block so that we would be in walking distance from their family. We were also a bit closer to our older daughter's family who were now four hours north in Wisconsin instead of five hours plus, and we were a little closer to our son's family who lived in the city of Chicago.

We enjoyed being in our new home and began attending services at the church where our daughter and son-in-law were attending. It was a large church, and although we enjoyed the services, I struggled with deciding where to serve. Eventually, I became content with being a consumer Christian and not serving in the church at all. I continued to be a part of the weekly Bible study at work, but didn't put much effort into looking for other opportunities. Besides, after the hour plus of commuting each way to work on weekdays, I was ready to rest.

Secret Sin \ Baermann

What about my habit? I hoped that you'd ask again. Well, I'd have to say that it was pretty much under control at that point, probably due more to the fact that I found little satisfaction in it more than any other reason.

It was on my commute home from work one afternoon that my life began to take an unexpected turn. I was tuned in to a program on the Christian radio station that I listened to each day when an interview with a gentleman who was describing his struggle with ALS (Lou Gehrig's disease) caught my attention. He described some early symptoms that were eerily similar to some issues that I had started to experience, such as occasional tripping and some slurring of my speech. I was fascinated by the story of how his faith was giving him strength to deal with the disease, but it scared me enough to make an appointment with my primary doctor.

My visit to the internist resulted in nothing more than a referral to a neurologist, who performed a cursory examination on me. He noted some minor issues, recommended a blood test, and told me to return in six months for a follow-up visit. My blood test didn't reveal anything abnormal except for elevated cholesterol levels, and after insignificant changes in my symptoms, my next appointment resulted in his recommendation of a form of nerve testing, which was performed shortly thereafter. The end result was the news that I probably didn't have ALS, but probably did have some of the early symptoms of Parkinson's disease. He scheduled me for follow-up and sent me on my way.

At this point, my diagnosis hadn't resulted in any lifestyle changes. I was still doing all of the things that I used to do with little difficulty. It was months later that I began to notice an increasing problem with walking and balance. With the onset of these increasing symptoms, I decided to seek a second opinion. So I scheduled an appointment with another neurologist in our area. After his initial examination, he confirmed the diagnosis of Parkinson's disease and prescribed a medication used in treating the early symptoms of the disease.

One morning on my way to work, as I was listening to my favorite station, I was confronted by an editorial about addictions. I use the word confronted because of the impact that it had on me when I heard the commentator's comments. Long story short, she was explaining how research had revealed how certain repeated behaviors can negatively impact the brain's pleasure centers and the part that dopamine plays in the process. Having read a bit about Parkinson's disease, I knew that the lack of dopamine in the brain was linked with the disease. Suddenly I was faced with the question of whether my habit had played a part in causing the disease that I was now battling. The possibility was devastating, and all but confirmed in my mind the reality of what I had only wondered about before.

You would think that the knowledge that I had gained, along with my body's inability to function sexually any longer, would have caused my habit to die a natural death. Unfortunately, "it" wasn't finished with me yet. Little did I know

6 \ What's Up Doc?

that the fight would escalate to a higher level. Even though I could no longer derive the satisfaction that was once enticing, I was suddenly experiencing the desire to do "it", and other impure thoughts began to assault my mind. I was to discover later that treatment of Parkinson's disease with some dopamine agonist medications may cause compulsive sexual behavior (you got to be kidding me).

After struggling with these thoughts and desires for several months, my disease suddenly worsened. It had progressed to the point where I needed to consider how long to continue working. I wish that I could say that my motivation was to play more golf, but by now my game had been affected to the extent that playing was now more of a struggle to drag myself around the course rather than a walk in the park. I was experiencing increased problems with walking and balance, small motor skills such as working at the computer, and tiredness. By now I had learned that my disease was an aggressive variant of Parkinsonism known as MSA, Multiple Systems Atrophy, which also affects the autonomic nervous system. I also found out that normally prescribed Parkinson's medications are ineffective in treating MSA. The symptoms eventually caused me to choose to quit working and apply for disability benefits through my employer. I also applied for disability benefits from Social Security.

I had heard horror stories about the length of time required for approval of Social Security disability benefits, and that it was normal to be denied benefits after initial application. Additionally, it was a real hassle dealing with the insurance company that administered my employer's disability program. After a couple of months of back and forth with the insurance company and finally getting approved, I was still awaiting notification from Social Security. About three months into the process, I got a letter from them. I was fully expecting a denial notification, but to my utter surprise it was an award letter. I had been approved, and the news literally brought me to tears. God had once again been incredibly good and extremely faithful to Barb and me. We *rejoiced* in the news, and I felt so unworthy of His blessing.

So What About…?

You may think that some of the questions that I was asking myself were rather strange given the fact that I was a believer; one whose faith was supposed to be in Christ and the sacrifice that He had made as payment for our sin. Maybe you think it to be unusual for me to wonder if my disease was linked to my behavior in some way, and I'm not saying that you're wrong. I'd ask you to consider these thoughts before you conclude that I was completely wrong for asking.

I had already determined that my continued practice of "it" was a sin (my conclusion based on my circumstances), and I perceived that God was not pleased by my behavior, especially after accepting Jesus as my Savior. Add to that my belief that all sin has natural consequences and that God has not promised to protect us from those consequences, and I'd hope that you can understand my reason for asking. I don't think that any of our questions are particularly wrong. It's the answers to those questions or our conclusions that sometimes can be wrong or misunderstood.

> What shall we say then? Are we to continue in sin that grace may abound? By no means! How can we who died to sin still live in it?
> —Romans 6:1-2, ESV

Repentance... or Consequences?

I THOUGHT THAT one of the advantages of being on disability would be having the chance to spend significantly more time studying the Bible, and in doing so I would become closer to God. What I quickly learned was that I had more time, but I wasn't really spending more time with Him, and the time spent didn't result in me feeling any closer than before. I wondered if the wall between us had something to do with the issue of repentance. I had confessed doing "it" more times than I could remember, but I hadn't turned from it. I had always dismissed my need to do this by convincing myself that repentance was all about changing my mind about getting to heaven by relying on my good works, to a reliance on Christ's work on the cross, and His sacrifice alone, to get me there. Of course, I had done that years before, but I obviously wasn't convinced that there wasn't more to it. I continued to wonder what part my continual sin had played in the onset and progression of my disease. What caused it? Did my wrong choices cause it? Did God cause it? Is He angry with me? Is He punishing me? Can there be any hope that He still cares about me? Will He rescue me from my presumed sure fate? I prayed that God would help me understand the truth of what His Word taught about repentance.

I'd say that it was within a week that I received my monthly copy of Today in the Word, a devotional from Moody Bible Institute, and guess what the theme for the month was. Repentance! I was suddenly energized by a sense that God had heard my prayer; in fact, He knew my need and was well ahead of me in meeting it. I was alive with anticipation over what He might teach me. What followed was a month of God pouring His grace (unmerited favor) into my heart by changing my focus from what I had done to what He will do; from dwelling on the past to hope in the future. Here is what I highlighted from my readings over the first three days.

> Day 1: Repentance involves transformation. It is not about the past, but the future. It is not focused on what we have done, but what God will do in us. It is not about God laying a guilt trip on us so much as it about God showing us how to be free from a past that enslaves us. This truly is good news.
>
> Day 2: God will send rescue, but only when we see Him, and not ourselves, in the midst of our pain. As scholar Kallistos Ware put it, 'To repent is to look, not downward at my own shortcomings, but upward at God's love. It is to see not what I have failed to do, but what by the grace of Christ I can yet become.'
>
> Day 3: When faced with our sin and the misery and destruction it caused, we may be tempted to despair. 'Darkness' may seem triumphant. Yet, this is just where God begins His work. Repentance can mean a new day for all of us. (*Today in the Word*, June 2011, Moody Bible Institute)

The month ended with me underlining this statement: "We are not alone in our temptations, and God has not abandoned us to our sin. We have Jesus promise to be with us always (Matt. 28:20) and His Holy Spirit as a pledge of our future inheritance (Ephesians 1:13-14)." After a month of following along with the study (and from this point forward I'll just refer to it as "the study"), I think that I had a greater understanding of repentance, but I know that I had a greater realization of and appreciation for God's love for me.

Here's what I think that I learned about repentance. I believe that it's always about our sin, and what we do with it. It starts by agreeing with God that we are sinners, and recognizing that (because we are sinners) we need Jesus. Although that recognition and confession determines our eternal destiny, because of the payment that He made on the cross, that isn't the end of repentance for us, but the beginning of a life of repenting and turning from various sins. In Christ, our eternal destiny is secure because of God's grace, but sin can affect the course of this life. I hope that God would say, "Yeah Rich, you got it right." Did He answer all of my questions about my disease? Well, let's see.

Let's start with these. Did God cause it? Is He angry with me? Is He punishing me?

7 \ Repentance… or Consequences?

In the book of Romans, the Bible tells us that everyone has sinned; we all fall short of God's glorious standard. Yet God, with undeserved kindness, declares that we are righteous. He did this through Christ Jesus when he freed us from the penalty for our sins. (Romans 3:23-24,NLT) We are sinners who are declared to be righteous. Why would God punish, or be angry with, someone whom He has declared righteous. As I studied, I struggled with the meaning of the words punishes, discipline, chastises, etc. that I found in various versions or translations. They seemed to be used interchangeably; yet, in my understanding they seemed to communicate differing feelings that God might have in dealing with us. The version that best communicated God's heart in the matter, for me, comes from The Message and says:

> It's the child he loves that he disciplines; the child he embraces, he also corrects. God is educating you; that's why you must never drop out. He's treating you as dear children. This trouble you're in isn't punishment; it's training, the normal experience of children. (Hebrews 12:6, 7, MSG)

The motivations of discipline, correction, and training just felt right in trying to understand God's heart for me and fit with the following comment that I found on day twenty-three of the study. "As often as you sin, repent of your sin. Do not despair….Do not by indifference lose hope of the good things prepared. For here is a physician's office, not a courtroom; not a place where punishment is exacted, but where forgiveness is granted. When we experience ongoing struggle with sin, we can still trust that Christ, the Great Physician, will bring healing." (*Today in the Word,* June 2011, Moody Bible Institute) What physician would knowingly cause illness? Christ, the Great Physician, has cured us of an illness that was certain to result in eternal *death,* and permanently healed us so that we will have eternal *life.* INCREDIBLE! Did God cause it? I'd say no.

If God didn't cause it, what did? Did my wrong choices cause it? Well, let's see what the Bible says. In Galatians we are told that "Those who live only to satisfy their own sinful nature will harvest decay and death from that sinful nature. But those who live to please the Spirit will harvest everlasting life from the Spirit." (Galatians 6:8, NLT) The English Standard Version (ESV) says it this way: "For the one who sows to his own flesh will from the flesh reap corruption, but the one who sows to the Spirit will from the Spirit reap eternal life." Decay and death (corruption) come from the sinful nature (the flesh), and eternal life comes from the Spirit. Living to satisfy the sinful nature is sin. If we sin, does this mean that we don't have eternal life, or if we have eternal life, does it mean we never sin? Well, the Bible also says that "If we claim we have no sin, we are only fooling ourselves and not living in the truth." (1 John 1:8, NLT) If we're living in the truth, we need to admit that we are still sinners; sinners that sometimes choose to satisfy our sinful nature. We need a Savior that not only has paid the penalty for our past sins, but for our present and future sins, and Jesus has done that.

If He hadn't, we'd be assured of going to heaven one day, and have no assurance the next. If we're trusting Jesus for our salvation, we can be assured that He has paid the penalty for all of our sins, not just some of them.

What happens when we, as ones who have put their faith in Christ, choose to satisfy our sinful nature, especially repeatedly, as I had? I had confessed my sin, and remember this verse that says "if we confess our sins to him, he is faithful and just to forgive us our sins and to cleanse us from all wickedness." (1 John 1:9, NLT) So I was forgiven, but I hadn't turned from my sin; I hadn't truly repented of "it". On day seventeen of the study there was this comment, "Without true repentance, the Israelites fell back into destructive habits." What was true of God's chosen people was also true of me, but "He looks for excuses to shower us with blessings." I've told you how God had blessed me and my family, and I'm sure that, over the years, He was looking for excuses on my behalf. Here are some more quotes from the study that served to help me answer my remaining questions.

- God will hand us over to the consequences of our own behavior. But such disasters are never what God truly wants for us.
- He seeks to save us from ourselves. We need to be reoriented in our walk with Him.
- Our God cared enough to pour out the judgment for our sin on His own Son to provide for us to be in relationship with Him. He cares enough to get our attention, to bring us back into fellowship.
- Suffering can be a call for us to repent, a call to realize that God loves us enough not to let us walk away.
- When we repent our downcast eyes will lead us heavenward, and 'those who will humble themselves will be exalted.'
- We cannot deny the misery our sin causes, but we must not stop there. We need a greater vision of how God can fill us with His love, even if we have walked away from Him. God still has work for us to do, and our repentance and His forgiveness prepare us to fellowship with Him and others.
- He offers us the blessing of His presence when we acknowledge our sin and repent.

Did my wrong choices cause it? Is my disease a consequence of my sin, or is it God's discipline? First, let me take you back to one of the verses that I quoted earlier that says, "It's the child he loves that he disciplines." (Hebrews 12:6, MSG) I hope that you've gotten the sense from all that I've shared with you from my study is that God's motivation in correcting His children is one of love.

Do you remember what I said about listening to a radio program on my way to work one morning that dealt with the negative effects of repeated behaviors on the pleasure centers of the brain? I've done a bit of research on how the brain

7 \ Repentance... or Consequences?

functions, and I think it's safe to say that, although much is understood, the chemical interactions that take place within it are so complex that even when understood, cannot always be reproduced. I'd imagine that it's also safe to say that no one can be absolutely sure of the effect that certain thoughts and actions will have on the brain over time. I do know that the chemical, dopamine, is associated with both the pleasure response and Parkinsonism, but what I don't know is whether or not masturbation can cause Parkinsonism. Even if that question were to be answered, I certainly wouldn't imply that everyone with a neurological disease has some sort of sin habit, or everyone with Parkinsonism struggles with masturbation.

I've already said that I don't believe that God caused my disease, but what's the answer to the discipline/consequence questions? I believe that my disease *is* a consequence of my behavior and God has used that consequence to save me from myself; to reorient me in my walk with Him. All of the other statements above are true as well. He has used it to get my attention because He cares, and has used the suffering to call me to repent because He still has work for me to do and He wants to bless me with His presence so that I can have fellowship with Him and others. I am absolutely convinced of the fact that He still cares about me! I can even say with confidence, HE LOVES ME! How will He answer my final question, will He rescue me from my presumed sure fate?

So What About...?

So what's the big deal about repentance stuff? Does it seem as complicated to you as it was to me? As you can see, I was asking allot of questions about the origins of my disease, and I managed to find answers to most. Your circumstances may be different, but the truths about repentance are universal.

I hope that no one accuses me of saying or implying that there is always a link between Parkinson's disease and masturbation. I never said that and never would. Never! Why? Because I don't believe that to be true. The question that I asked was a very personal one about there being a link between the practice and the disease in my case. The answer that I reached was that it was a possibility in my case; a possibility that may or not be true scientifically. Nevertheless, I believe my God is sovereign and is able to use any circumstance for His purposes.

I mentioned that this should be a life of repenting and turning from various sins. First, there has to be a time when agree with God that we are sinners and about His provision through Christ being the only way of salvation (repent of our sinfulness) and then we need to repent of the sins we commit (repent of our sins) by confessing and turning from them (at least have the intention of never committing them again).

I said that I hadn't truly repented of my sin, and someone may ask whether our obedience must be lifelong for it to be authentic? In addition to what I just said I'd say that it doesn't *have* to be lifelong, thanks to our wonderful Savior, but we shouldn't treat it as a license to sin again. Confession without a desire to stop the offending action is little more than just that: confession. We are agreeing with God that we have sinned, but we have no desire, no plan to stop (I just can't, I don't want to, I know it's wrong but that's just the way I am, etc.).

What does that mean to you and me? Once we agree with God and trust Christ for our salvation our sins are forgiven and we're on our way to heaven. Of course, if you deny the fact that you have sinned, you're on your way to hell. If you have trusted Christ for your salvation and confess your sins but don't repent, you may still experience the natural consequences of your sin. That fact emphasizes the importance of repentance for the believer's growth and assurance of salvation.

During the writing of this book, God taught me subsequent to my study of repentance what should have been obvious to me early on. I should have realized it because I experienced it over and over again. That truth is that confession is not the same as repentance. We shouldn't be surprised if nothing changes if all we do is confess without a heart that is repentant as well. The truth that I want you to remember if it's not obvious to you already is this:

Repentance > Confession

> If we say that we have no sin, we deceive ourselves, and the truth is not in us.
> —1 John 1:8, KJV

> Who then is the one who condemns? No one. Christ Jesus who died — more than that, who was raised to life — is at the right hand of God and is also interceding for us.
> —Romans 8:34, NIV

What Do You Call "It"?

I'M GOING to depart from my story for a moment to address the issue of sin and why man's heart is described as desperately wicked. (Jeremiah 17:9, KJV) There's a notion going around that, as children of God, we deserve certain things from Him simply because He is our Father, and all that we have to do is ask Him for them and they will be ours. It's referred to as "Name It and Claim It Theology." I have a problem with that kind of thinking, but I do think that we can expect certain things from Him simply because He is our Father and He is good. However, His conditional promises tell us what we should expect when we follow His instruction and if we fail to follow it as well. We will not always want what we deserve. What we deserve are not usually the blessings that they have in mind; blessings are usually the undeserved gifts of a loving God and are displayed in His grace to us.

This chapter is more about our ability to discern whether a particular action is a sin or not; to name "it" (identify it as God does) and then claim "it" (admit that you're guilty as charged). You can't expect to become more like Christ if you aren't in agreement with Him about sin. Yet He is more than gracious to us when we fail to agree. Do you remember His words? "Father, forgive them, for they do not know what they are doing." (Luke 23:34, NIV) I made a statement early on in the Acknowledgements section that has turned out to be so very true. It was this: I am extremely grateful that we have a God of not only second chances, but many, many more chances who can redeem the sorriest of circumstances that we have created through our disobedience of Him and glorify Himself while forgiving and blessing us in the process.

Let me begin by saying that I think that the Christian community needs to begin this or any discussion with an attitude of love, not judgment. Only our righteous God has the authority to judge sin. We should be able to recognize it when it exists, to discern right from wrong, but our Savior's response to our sin problem was love, and that is where we should start. I don't think that I can even imagine the depth of a love that commands me to love your enemies and pray for those who persecute you (Matthew 5:44, NIV), but He demonstrated that kind of love to me and I need show that kind of love to others that I come in contact with.

We've already established early on that the word masturbation isn't found anywhere in the Bible. Some would say that's proof enough for them that it's not a sin. Some would say that the act Onan committed in Genesis 38 was the same thing, but others would interpret his sin as refusing to follow God's law.

> Then Judah said to Er's brother Onan, "Go and marry Tamar, as our law requires of the brother of a man who has died. You must produce an heir for your brother."
>
> But Onan was not willing to have a child who would not be his own heir. So whenever he had intercourse with his brother's wife, he spilled the semen on the ground. This prevented her from having a child who would belong to his brother. But the LORD considered it evil for Onan to deny a child to his dead brother. So the LORD took Onan's life, too. (Genesis 38:8-10, NLT)

Based on that evidence, you might conclude that God doesn't have an opinion regarding masturbation, but I still have my suspicions. I would maintain that as sinful human beings we're pretty good at being soft on sin anyway, and we're not much harder on it and don't readily agree when He says that it is. For example, let's look at the sin of homosexuality. The only reason that I'm bringing it up is for the purpose of including it as part of the larger issue of sexual sin and its pernicious nature.

Unlike masturbation, the word homosexuality *is* found in the Bible. I did a Keyword Search on it in using biblegateway.com's New International Version of the Bible and it turned up one verse. That verse is 1 Timothy 1:10 and here's what it says in context with verses nine and eleven:

> We also know that the law is made not for the righteous but for lawbreakers and rebels, the ungodly and sinful, the unholy and irreligious, for those who kill their fathers or mothers, for murderers, for the

8 \ What Do You Call "It"?

sexually immoral, for those practicing homosexuality, for slave traders and liars and perjurers—and for whatever else is contrary to the sound doctrine that conforms to the gospel concerning the glory of the blessed God, which he entrusted to me.

What I'd like you to notice is that homosexuality is a sin that's in a class by itself to most of us, yet it is not listed first here but later in the list, and is listed with sins that we might think are as seemingly small as lying. This seems to confirm the fact that any sin is enough to condemn us and needs to be forgiven. What's amazing is Christ's death and resurrection is always sufficient payment for any sin, from one as seemingly innocent as a white lie to one that was so horrendous to the Father that the cities where this sin was practiced have become the poster children for judgment by fire and brimstone because of the sin of their inhabitants.

It was at about this point in the original rewriting of chapter (which was added as a result of a need to address some issue that I no longer have a clear recollection of) that I began to go astray. In an effort to point out some things that were true of homosexuals and their sin, I had changed the focus from my secret sin to an editorial about them. Though it all may have been true, instead of accomplishing my objective of trying to emphasize the serious nature of all sin by magnifying my sin and minimizing theirs I had done exactly what I had admonished us not to do; I had begun to judge those who I should be trying to reach for Christ.

I also noticed that I had not heard from some of the key members of my support/review group since I had sent out my latest revisions, and suddenly it seemed as though I was having problems with the last few items that needed to be done prior to publishing. It was during one of my sleepless nights that have become a blessing of late that God revealed the source of my problem. Due to my incontinence, I had begun to use a product that, let's say, caused me to spend moments on an area that was not good for me to focus upon, and my thoughts were still not always pure, even after all this adversity. It wasn't as though the product caused the problem; it simply revealed the condition of my still desperately wicked heart. Just because I wasn't sinning to the extent that I had been didn't mean that I wasn't sinning. I hadn't confessed it by calling it sin and repented because I was still much too willing to be soft on sin. This was an issue of purity, and God, because He is faithful, would not allow me to move forward with these issues unresolved.

I've reached the point where I ask the question, "Is any other sin really any worse than mine?" Let's spend some time examining it. You might say that we aren't sure whether mine was a sin, and I'd tell you that I'm way past using that argument to rationalize it away. I think that there is enough evidence to say that I needed Jesus. I think I concluded that there are cases where it may not be a sin, but there are plenty of cases where it is. That may still leave you in the place of asking, is it or isn't it? Are you satisfied with my answer that it could be both? If you are, you need to ask yourself some difficult questions.

The sinister part of the practice of masturbation is that, because nothing is said about it in Scripture, we are left to decide if and when it is a sin. There is no other practice that is more indicative of our heart condition than this one because we are the judge. It's our opportunity to decide what sin is and whether it needs to be confessed. Maybe the question that we need to ask ourselves is whether we could possibly imagine Jesus ever doing "it"? I know that I can't. I can't imagine that Jesus, who is our example of purity, would ever commit what I view as a self-centered act. If our answer to that question is "NEVER", we might be able to come to some conclusion for our own conduct. Does our heart beat with God's on the subject? Are we as sensitive to sin as He is? If our objective was purity, what would we call it?

So What About...?

What about the question of how you're supposed to know if this or that is a sin? Well, we all have our own opinions anyway, and did you really think that He has to tell us (yes, but not in the ways you might think)? Consider this verse:

> Even Gentiles, who do not have God's written law, show that they know his law when they instinctively obey it, even without having heard it. They demonstrate that God's law is written in their hearts, for their own conscience and thoughts either accuse them or tell them they are doing right. (Romans 2:14-15, NLT)

So the excuse of "I didn't know" just isn't going to fly with God. Sorry! Claiming you didn't know if what you did or didn't do was right or wrong isn't an excuse. You know the first time you do "it" (whatever your "it" is) whether it is a sin or not. If it is, and you continue to ignore the voice of your conscience, His voice will get weaker and weaker until, unless you have been saved by God's amazing grace, you will no longer be able to hear it.

> For although they knew God, they did not honor him as God or give thanks to him, but they became futile in their thinking, and their foolish hearts were darkened. Claiming to be wise, they became fools, (Romans 1:20-22, ESV)

I feel as though the point at which "it" becomes a sin is when it starts to be a "me-centered" act, which for me was all the time. Another indicator would be when "it" ceases to be done as part of God's will for my life and becomes a selfish I will, which was all the time for me as well. If you could do "it" for the benefit of someone else and without committing another sin in the process, there may be reason to believe that you haven't sinned, but if there is even a hint of sin and doubt in your mind and if your desire is purity, I'd be careful. All who have this hope in him purify themselves, just as he is pure. (James 3:3, NIV) He tells us, Be holy because I am holy. (1 Peter 1:16) His standard is always to go above and beyond (anger=murder, looking lustfully=adultery, etc.); we lean toward doing the minimum. Why is that? Could the answer be that we don't *trust* God enough to believe that the benefit of doing things *His Way* outweighs anything that we can imagine?

> Although they know God's righteous decree that those who do such things deserve death, they not only continue to do these very things but also approve of those who practice them.
> —Romans 1:32, NIV

> You, therefore, have no excuse, you who pass judgment on someone else, for at whatever point you judge another, you are condemning yourself, because you who pass judgment do the same things.
> —Romans 2:1, NIV

Secret Sin \ Baermann

Whom Do You Trust?

I WOKE UP very early this morning, as I am prone to do occasionally, and peered across the room to see the alarm clock reading 2:34 a.m. It was then that my mind began to race with thoughts about this chapter. You see, I had already decided to delete a chapter that I had long since written called "Take Action". I had added it because I hadn't recommended a course of action to pursue to gain victory over habitual sin, and I thought that I should suggest something even though I hadn't traveled that path myself. So I suggested something that left me feeling uncomfortable when it was finished. This chapter was to take its place, but hadn't been developed as yet. God filled my mind with thoughts on the subject, but since once I get in bed at night I am basically unable to move without assistance, I began to wonder how in the world I would remember them without the ability to get them typed out on the computer. My penmanship is so bad that it's not an option either. After trying to commit them to memory, I finally decided that I would just have to trust God to help me to remember what He wanted me to say.

TRUST—I can't think of something that we do so much of, yet forget to do so often. I invite you to take some time to give it some thought; make a list of things you just assume will happen. Yet, in some instances where trust is required we come up woefully short. When it comes to our relationship with God, trust is a must. In fact, that sounds like it would make a good bumper sticker, "TRUST is a MUST." A lack of trust ruined our relationship with Him in the first place and only trust in Him can restore it. Adam and Eve's sin of mistrusting God ended up infecting the whole human race. Humans would forever require Jesus' sacrifice to redeem them, and consequently require us to "believe" and put our trust in Him and the sufficiency of His payment for our sin.

The need to trust in Jesus in order to be saved from our sin isn't the end, but the beginning of a life of trusting in the Spirit within us to help us turn from our sins. Salvation is a three step process of TRUST.

- Steps 1: Justification—*Trusting* in Christ to save us from the PENALTY of sin the moment we put our faith in Him: He takes on our sin and gives us His righteousness.
- Step 2: Sanctification—*Trusting* in the Spirit to save us from the POWER of sin: lifelong process of becoming more Christ-like through His Spirit.
- Step 3: Glorification—*Trusting* in the Father to save us from the PRESENCE of sin: eternal life will be ours in the sin-free environment of heaven at the time appointed by the Father because of the sufficiency of Christ's sacrifice for us.

Justification involves a one-time action on our part and glorification happens after our death (if we've been justified). It is the process of sanctification that involves commitment and sometimes a lifetime of struggle on our part. It involves cooperation between us and the Holy Spirit, and our success depends on our obedience to God's Word, on our attitude toward sin (repentance), on our dependence on the *power* of the Holy Spirit, and our *trust* that we are all that the Father has made us through Christ. God is perfectly committed to it and assures us that it *will* happen, because if we truly have been justified, He will glorify us. "And I am sure of this, that he who began a good work in you will bring it to completion at the day of Jesus Christ" (Philippians 1:6, ESV). We determine the speed and depth of our progress by how we respond to the Holy Spirit who encourages us toward repentance. If He's going to glorify those that have been justified anyway, why do we have to go through the process of sanctification? Well, we have to learn to value what He wants more than what we want. I'm not exactly sure how we go through the process will affect our eternity, but I am sure that it will affect us in this life.

What does all this have to do with your problem you might ask? Well, here's why I believe that I struggled for so long to gain victory over "it" and why I am at the place in life that I am right now. It's all because God is FAITHFUL. "Oh c'mon!" you say. You said that the chapter you've deleted recommended a course of action that I could pursue to have victory over habitual sin and now you're leaving me with this? You see, after all these years I'm still a work-in-progress, and God is still attempting to teach me what He wants me to learn. What I think that He's teaching me, and what I'm beginning to understand, is His work in my life.

I believe that God truly did start a good work in me many years ago. I was justified when I believed in who Jesus is and what He had done for me, and had trusted in Him as my personal Savior. I truly believed that I had been saved, that my sins had been forgiven, and that He had paid the cost of my salvation for me and I was on my way to heaven. I expected things to change, but when they didn't I confessed my failure to God, as I've already mentioned. Unfortunately, confession didn't change my actions, and after a while I began to wonder if I ever would change. I began to *feel* like a failure. I began to *feel* as though God was becoming tired of forgiving my continuing sin and I certainly didn't *feel* like I was purified.

I have already recounted my attempts to fix my problem myself or to find someone who would fix it for me; the confessions to various people, the search for an accountability partner, the visits to a counselor, and the participation in a recovery group. All proved ineffective when it came to helping me to claim victory over my sin. I've come to believe that the source of my struggle was misplaced trust; not a lack of trust in Christ's work, but a lack of understanding of what I had gained as a result of my trust in Christ, and a lack of reliance on the Holy Spirit's power to change me. I was attempting to change by following *Man's Way* instead of *God's Way*. I was living my life on the basis of the lies of *feelings* instead of the *truth* of Scripture. I was continuing to rely on the inadequate resources of man's understanding, my wisdom, and my strength to gain victory over "it". I was living life without appropriating the power of the Spirit to eliminate "it" from my life that was mine as a result of having trusted in Christ, and I was experiencing the consequences of slavery instead of the gaining victory over my sin.

Sanctification is ultimately a team process, but it's a team of two; you and the Holy Spirit. Imagine that you are playing on a two person basketball team. You're a point guard and the Spirit's a power forward. Your coach, the Father, has developed a game plan that relies on the Spirit's ability. You have one assignment; to get the ball to Him. If you execute according to the plan, you will win. The key is to trust the Spirit with the ball. If you don't execute, and insist upon shooting instead of passing, you're going to lose. Without Him you're going to *lose* the game; you just won't realize it until it's too late. One game, one test, might be sufficient in some cases, but God will allow you to go through the same test over and over again until you learn that choosing *His Way* is best.

I hope that you get the idea that it's *all* about the issue of trust, but I want to make sure that you understand it as I am defining it. I view trust as a higher level of belief. I guess I'd define belief as head knowledge, intellectual assent, and trust as soul knowledge, spiritual reliance. I may be splitting hairs here, I know. Maybe I could put it another way; belief vs. BELIEF. I know that belief and faith are interchangeable throughout most of the Bible, but allow me to use two verses to explain what I mean. James 2:19 (NIV) states, You believe that there is one God. Good! Even the demons believe that—and shudder., and Romans 4:5 (NIV) tells us, However, to the one who does not work but trusts God who justifies the ungodly, their faith is credited as righteousness. So I would say that trusting in someone or something is more akin to having faith. I can believe something to be true without staking my life on it.

Trusting > Believing

What have I learned from my experience that I would hope to pass on to you? What can I tell you that you should and shouldn't do to help you experience victory in the process of becoming who we already are in Christ, as I describe it, since you are going to be involved in it multiple times each day for the rest of your life? I guess that it's really pretty simple, but as with many things in life we tend to make it a lot harder than it has to be. First, grab hold of a couple of verses and trust that they're true of you right now (if you've trusted Christ as your Savior).

> Therefore, if anyone is in Christ, he is a new creation. The old has passed away; behold, the new has come. (2 Corinthians 5:17, ESV)

> So you also must consider yourselves dead to sin and alive to God in Christ Jesus. (Romans 6:11, ESV)

Now, let me suggest some things to remember when those thoughts that you seem to have been struggling with forever cross your mind; when you're faced with a choice between going *God's Way* or *Man's Way*. Don't think, "'I wonder if this is a test from God or temptation from Satan?" The answer to both of those questions is yes! We must understand that at times God draws an unseen circle around us and within that circle the Accuser comes in to entice us. We are tempted to step outside of the circle of God's unseen protection into the certainty of loss, turmoil, and destruction. However we must remember that God himself abides within us. He has not left us to ourselves. The Lord himself surrounds every test and every temptation waiting expectantly to see what decision we will make. He is truly transforming us into likeness of his Son." (trenidydavis.com 1/21/13)

REJECT the LIES

- That you have no choice as to how you will act. Acting without *choosing* is acting without *thinking*.
- That the path you choose *doesn't* matter.
- That you are the *only one* that's faced this particular problem.

- That you are the *only one* affected by the choice you make.
- That you are *powerless* to change or alone in your struggle.
- That you are *unloved* or *unlovable* when you fail.
- That you may as well *give up* if you don't experience positive results

TRUST in the TRUTH

- That you should identify the choices and choose *God's Way* before acting.
- That the path you choose *does* matter.
- That others have faced the *same* struggle that you are facing.
- That others *will* be affected by your choice if you continue to make the wrong one.
- That the Holy Spirit *will* help you if you allow Him to.
- That if you *fail,* you're not a *failure* because of Jesus' completed work. Confess your sin and carry on *trusting.*
- That *success* is yours through your FAITH in Christ.

Those are seven LIES and TRUTHS to REJECT or BELIEVE that I can recommend from my experience. If you can think of any of them when faced with a choice, you're probably ahead of the game, but of all of them the first LIE and the last TRUTH are the most critical. THINK and TRUST; THINK before you act and choose *God's Way,* and TRUST that the victory is yours already through the power of the Spirit. There are a couple of things to remember about sanctification; you can't sanctify yourself and you can't sanctify someone else, no matter how much you'd like to try. Remember, sanctification is ultimately a team process, and it's a team of two; you and the Holy Spirit. You won't experience success going it alone, and you dare not try to take the Spirit's place in someone else's life. Do you think that you can do a better job than *He* can? If you become disappointed with someone's progress after having instructed and encouraged them, how do you think God feels when our choices cause us to have to suffer?

Having grandchildren has given me a whole new perspective on some things. For example: I think that sometimes, as fathers, we have greater expectations for our children than our Heavenly Father has for them; especially considering their age. Jesus says that His "…yoke is easy, and my burden is light. (Matthew 11:30, KJV), so it's got to be light enough for a child to carry, yet we expect them to have learned everything that we have learned and expect them to be ready to learn the same things that we're learning. In our passion to instruct and protect them, do we ever consider the possibility that we can frustrate them by making them carry burdens that are too heavy for them?

I know that the Bible tells us, Train up a child in the way he should go; even when he is old he will not depart from it (Proverbs 22:6, KJV), but I think that this means less about giving them a set of rules to follow than teaching them that Jesus is the *Way* that they should go. It's about following Jesus, not rules; teaching them that Jesus loves them and that deciding to trust Him is the *best* decision that they can possibly make. We need to encourage them to love Him by loving Him ourselves, and then pray for that reality to come to pass and trust that it will. We don't want them to grow-up too fast in other ways, but is it possible that we can be asking them to grow up too fast spiritually? We fail to realize that God will be FAITHFUL to them, as He has been FAITHFUL to us, if we all will just TRUST Him.

Becoming who we already are in Christ; it's also the process of making our faith our experience. You've heard that what you think about yourself determines who you become; well in this case it's more like what you trust to be true about yourself determines how you'll act. It's about trusting that what God has said about us is true and actually living that way. It's about actually experiencing the life that God wants for us. There isn't a question that is more important that can be asked than "WHOM DO YOU TRUST?

It's finally time to recommend that course of action to pursue to gain victory over habitual sin that I talked about at the beginning of the chapter (this time I can do it with a clear conscience). First, let me point you to a place on the web where you can go and not feel alone in your struggle. It's www.allaboutlifechallenges.org. It doesn't matter what kind of issue that you're dealing with, they've got it covered. Next, if you've got questions regarding your faith, I'd look at a website that will help you understand the truth of the Bible and, in so doing, the truth about yourself. That website is www.gracewalk.org, an outreach of Grace Walk Ministries and Dr. Steve McVey. There you will find what you need to understand if you are to have hope of finding victory over your addiction. There's also a book that I can recommend that he's written with a gentleman by the name of Mike Quarles that you need to read if you're someone who's attempting to help someone else with their addiction entitled "Helping Others Overcome Addiction". I know that if you can understand the truths that you will find there, you will be well on your way to finding victory in whatever area you are struggling with.

So What About…?

I mentioned that I had tried "to *fix* my problem myself or to find someone who would *fix* it for me" and "I didn't *feel* purified". I should have known that sinners cannot fix sin. Without the help of the Holy Spirit I would never be fixed, and without repentance I would never experience His power to purify me.

There is a whole other dimension after salvation. Salvation is just the first step in the journey of becoming and experiencing what God had intended for you before you were born. Trust that He is *for* you, knows what's best for you, and is the only One that is capable of making all of His plans a reality for you.

Whoever puts his trust in His Son is not guilty. Whoever does not put his trust in Him is guilty already. It is because he does not put his trust in the name of the only Son of God.

—John 3:18, NLV

Secret Sin \ Baermann

Collateral Damage

I'VE MENTIONED it before in passing, but I hadn't realized what a glaring omission I had made until I asked my wife to proofread what I had written. While she indicated that she thought what had been said was well written, there was something of great meaning to her that I had failed to emphasize, the extent to which my addiction had affected her and our marriage. OUCH! I thought that I knew how deeply I had wounded her, but I had once again failed to give it the significance it deserved or mention the overall part it had played in shaping our relationship and molding her into the person that she was.

The title of this chapter resulted from the fact that I didn't set out to harm anyone. Collateral damage is the unintended harm that's caused to civilians and their possessions as a result of an attack on a military target. I certainly didn't decide to destroy anyone else's life, least of all my wife's, but by persisting in my pursuit of self-satisfaction I had failed to meet her needs, and that failure caused irreparable damage to her being. I had fallen short of fulfilling my obligation to meet her physical, emotional, and spiritual needs, and although I've already been forgiven by God for that sin and every other sin I've ever committed or will commit, I will have to give account of my actions one day. Needless to say, I had almost failed to include some of the most important things that I can say to you and that you need to consider. So I'm dedicating this chapter to her and recognizing that her faithfulness throughout the personal pain she has suffered has been most honoring to God (and to me) and deserves praise beyond what I can give, but that I hope she will receive in full measure from her Lord and Savior, Jesus Christ. She has absorbed many blows for the greater good of our family, and her commitment to our marriage has protected them from additional suffering.

I've talked a lot about my disease and some of the hardship I've had to suffer, but I need to share some of the personal hardship that she has suffered because I failed to love her as I should. My disease has gradually stolen my ability to have sexual relations and I wasn't very good at finding other ways to meet her sexual needs. I don't know, but I'd suspect, that if that alone had been the problem, she may have been able to handle it with less suffering. Coupled with the issue of virtually non-existent sexual intimacy was a lack of emotional intimacy. She would say that we spent very little meaningful time together just being close, sharing our thoughts and feelings with each other. On top of that, we weren't spending time with God together, thus spiritual intimacy between us was lacking as well. I had allowed the One who had united us in marriage to be left out of the equation, and that omission was causing us to drift apart. The combination of these three failures on my part created a deadly cocktail that caused her to act in ways that she probably wouldn't have had if had she not been forced to drink of it daily. Oh, if I could only help you realize that how the way you live your life affects those around you dramatically. Your life is *not* lived in a vacuum or a bubble that protects others from being infected by the toxin of your sin. You've heard that one rotten apple spoils the whole bushel; similarly, it's why the sin of one man, Adam, infected the whole human race. All are affected negatively by it; no one can escape the effects of its poison.

It pains me to see my wife angry, short-tempered, lacking patience at times, living with a "glass that is half-empty" attitude, while always wondering how I had contributed negatively to the person she had become. Every time she cared for me in a less than pleasant way, was abrupt in action or tone, or became impatient with me and displayed anger with me when problems arose or when there was some *crisis* in her life (which was virtually everything that didn't go her way), I couldn't help thinking that I was reaping the fruit of all those years that she had been starved of intimacy. The fact that she is still caring for me at all gives testimony to her faithfulness. Some of you would say that she should be considered a saint in the world's estimation, as she already is in God's because Jesus gave up His life for her.

Of course, each of us is ultimately responsible for our own sin. Each of us chooses the way we react to the failures of others to treat us as they should. None of us can point to someone else and blame them for our shortcomings. None of us should expect perfect love from imperfect human beings. If we do, we will always be setting ourselves up for disappointment. The *only* One who can love perfectly is our Lord, and He is the One we should look to for fulfillment when others disappoint us. What I'm attempting to say is, while I don't take full responsibility for her actions, I had failed to fulfill the responsibilities that God requires of me as a husband.

Another point that I need to emphasize, if I haven't said it already, is that there is no such thing as a secret sin. Only those to whom I had confessed "it" knew of mine, and had I not confessed it to them, no one would have known, humanly speaking. You may succeed in keeping it hidden for a time, but you can't keep it from affecting you, from changing you, and from ultimately affecting others. Even if you were able to hide it from everyone on the planet, never interacted with anyone, and were able to take your secret to the grave with you, if you are naive enough to think that possibility exists, its effect on you would still be devastating, if no one else. Your sin will *always* find you out, for nothing is a secret to an all-knowing God. Your offense is ultimately an offense against Him. Only He can restore it.

So, what about...? There are some who would say that I lack a deep understanding of the pain that Barb experienced as a result of my actions. I would readily agree that I don't fully understand and I don't know if I ever will. I suppose that may sound like a cop-out to some of you, and to be honest with you, it could be. I've just given-up trying to decide which of her actions that I need to take responsibility for and which is hers. I know that's not the way things should be, so I guess that you say that I'm still struggling in that area. So I'd ask that you'd pray that I'd be sensitive to God's leading and to my wife in the midst of our circumstances.

> **For the wages of sin is death, but the gift of God is eternal life in Christ Jesus our Lord.**
> **—Romans 6:22-23, NIV**

Secret Sin \ Baermann

Choices

OKAY. SINCE you're still reading, I have to ask where you stand with all this God talk? What about sin? Maybe you're thinking that I've taken something that's normal and made *way* too big a deal of it. Maybe you think that I've got some mental issues to go along with my physical problems. Maybe you're just wondering what I'll say next.

I don't know what you think of my story, but in the final analysis, all of our stories are the same. Each and every one of us has been condemned by our conscience about something we've done. Is your conscience still speaking to you? Remember this verse: For everyone has sinned; we all fall short of God's glorious standard. (Romans 3:23, NLT) The Bible also says that what we'll receive as a result of those actions is death; For the wages of sin is death... (Romans 6:23a, NLT), but the rub is that we don't just close our eyes for the last time and cease to exist. We're all headed somewhere after we die and we're going to be there forever. If you had your choice, which would you choose; a horribly bad place, or an unbelievably good place? Let me put it this way. Where would you rather own a condo; the Sahara Desert or Hawaii? More importantly, who would you rather spend your (eternal) life with; someone who loves you (Jesus), or someone who hates you (Satan)? The good news is that you *do* have a choice. You can choose to accept God's gift; For the wages of sin is death, but the free gift of God is eternal life through Christ Jesus our Lord. (Romans 6:23, NLT) You just have to do what Barb and I did that night in our dining room. You have to admit that you are a sinner (repent) and receive the gift that God is offering to you.

If you've received God's gift, but have a habit that continues to enslave you, there is a choice for you to make as well. You can choose to continue to practice your habit and risk the possibility of experiencing the consequences of doing so, or you can choose to trust that victory is yours with the help of the Spirit, whose power is available to you through Christ, and you can repent of (turn from) that sin and experience the reward that accompanies obedience. You can choose to change direction; to start heading down the road that leads to freedom and get off of the road that enslaves you. Do you recall this quote from my *Repentance* study? "God will hand us over to the consequences of our own behavior, but such disasters are never what God truly wants for us." (*Today in the Word*, June 2011, Moody Bible Institute)

I've told you my story, and although I can't be absolutely sure that all that I've said is true, I know that God, in love, has used my disease to call me to repentance. God has allowed this in my life even though it appeared that I followed all of the rules, by the world's standards. The question for you is this: what consequences are you willing to risk having to endure as a result of your repeated sin? What will it take for you to gain a greater vision of God's love for you? He still has work for you to do, and will offer you the blessing of His presence if you'll repent.

On day 4 of the study, I underlined these words: "We can make no new beginning with God unless we see that all we can bring is our tired and broken self to Him. God knows our weakness, and He will not ask for more than we can give." On day 8 there was this: "Repentance is not about our sin, but God's grace. We ourselves may never repent unless we realize that no sin is beyond God's forgiveness, and none of us is beyond Christ's redemption. Nothing this day should keep us from the throne of grace."

If you've never put your trust in Jesus, and Him alone, for your salvation, it is my prayer that you wouldn't put it off any longer. Today can be the day that you can have the assurance of *knowing* you're going to heaven when you die. And if you've put your faith in what He has done for you, but you're struggling with a habit that has caused you to feel unworthy of His love, I pray that today will be the day that you repent and restore your fellowship with Him. Change your direction and change your future. It is my hope that you will choose the right path; the path that leads you toward joy and peace and away from heartache and pain.

But whoever looks intently into the perfect law that gives freedom, and continues in it—not forgetting what they have heard, but doing it—they will be blessed in what they do.

—James 1:25, NIV

Secret Sin \ Baermann

Blessings in Disguise

MY SON-IN-LAW frequently has this little thing that he does with my granddaughter before praying for a meal. You may have heard it before. It goes like this: he'll say, "God is good", and she'll respond, "All the time". Then he'll say, "All the time", and she'll respond, "God is good". It's a good way of remembering and reinforcing the sometimes doubted truth that He is ALWAYS good, not just some of the time.

Laura Story's song *Blessings* poses the question, "What if trials of this life are Your mercies in disguise?" (*Blessings,* Words and music by Laura Story 2011) God's Word assures us, …that in all things God works for the good of those who love him, who have been called according to his purpose (Romans 8:28, NIV), but that verse always begged another question for me: *Do I really love God?* I would suppose that anyone who is trusting in Christ for their salvation would say that they wished that they loved God more. Speaking for myself, His blessings have always been more about His perfect love for me than my puny love for Him. It's been that way from the start: But God demonstrates his own love for us in this: While we were still sinners, Christ died for us. (Romans 5:8, NIV)

I can personally testify of His mercies being evident in the midst of my trial. Allow me to recount a few. I can recall a number of instances where God protected me from physical harm or turned my pride into demonstrations of His grace. I've already mentioned that a major issue of my disease has been poor balance, resulting in a tendency to fall.

One of those instances occurred on a Friday morning, shortly after Barb had left to attend a weekend conference. My daughter, who lived down the street was available in case I needed anything, and my son-in-law and my granddaughters were to spend the weekend with me starting later that day. I was headed over to a chair in the family room after having eaten breakfast when I fell. I landed on my gluteus maximus (rump, buttocks, fanny, call it what you wish) after just missing the corner of the wall with my head. The fall didn't result in any injury (God's protection), but I landed in an area where it was difficult to get up. I needed to find something to grab onto so that I could pull myself up, so I dragged myself over to the nearby staircase, hoping to use the handrail to lift myself. After expending a considerable amount of time, I was still unable to stand, and I had used up a significant amount of energy in the process. I had my cell phone in my pocket, and I could have called my daughter for help, but I didn't want anyone to know that I had fallen because I didn't want to ruin Barb's weekend. If she knew, I thought she might second-guess her choice to leave me alone or, worse yet, return home. Instead, I looked for another option. I decided to drag myself about ten feet down the hall into the living room and attempt to use the couch to stand. It was then that my cell phone rang. It was my daughter calling to check up on me. I answered my phone while I lay there in the floor, and told her that I was fine. Yeah, I did! Do you think I'd lie to you? You don't need to answer.

Well, I made it to the living room and attempted to right myself with no success, just a further sapping of my energy. After a total of approximately two hours of struggle, I was wiped out. I can hear you saying, serves you right, you LIAR. I suppose that I deserved whatever consequences I would suffer. As I lay on the floor trying to recover a bit of energy, I heard a voice. No, it wasn't God (or was it?). The voice was coming from my cell phone, which was now underneath me. It was my brother-in- law, now the pastor of a church in Puerto Rico, the one who started us on our *faith* journey. It had taken a while for me to answer, and he was asking if I was alright. Since he could tell by the sound of my voice that something was obviously wrong, I decided to confess that I had fallen. He had no idea how long I had been struggling to get up, and I didn't volunteer that information because I knew he would think it was pretty stupid of me not to call for help sooner. He asked if I was okay, and if I needed him to call someone. I said that I was, and I could easily call my daughter for help. So I finally called her and she came to my assistance. End of story. Not quite. Here's the INCREDIBLE part; GOD's amazing part.

When I heard that voice from my cell phone, I didn't know who it was until I picked it up and realized who was calling. What I didn't realize until later was that the phone never rang. I had called *him! He* was responding to my call.

12 \ Blessings in Disguise

It wasn't until after I had given it some thought that I discovered how incredible that was. You see, I had a double lock on my phone, and NO numbers set on speed dial. I needed to make a minimum of *five* specific keystrokes, in a specific order, some for a specific duration or successive presses, without contacting any other keys, to complete that call. I think that the miraculous call was God's way of telling me to give-it-up; to reach out for some help, for my own health and safety. It's just like God to offer to exchange the bad stuff that we deserve for the good stuff that we don't deserve.

There have been numerous instances of God's protection during falls; near misses where I came very close to hitting my head on the corner of a wall. I have also developed an uncanny ability to turn during my falls so that I land on my buttocks. I don't know how it happens; it just happens (ah-ha). But one major incident in particular gave evidence of His protection from physical harm. I had laid down for a nap in our upstairs bedroom and had set my phone on my walker next to the bed. I was awakened by a call and I sat up to answer it. The caller asked me a question that required Barb's input, so I stood up to go over to the staircase so that I could yell downstairs and get her answer. The next thing I knew, I was being helped up off the floor and the paramedics were arriving. I had fainted, knocking a small table into the room wall and damaging the wall in the process. A few minutes later, I was taking my first ride to the hospital in an ambulance, where I stayed for three days while the doctors attempted to discover why I had blacked-out. Fortunately, my fall had resulted in just a minor scrape under my left eye, and the incident was attributed to a drop in my blood pressure, likely associated with a condition known as orthostatic hypotension, which is associated with MSA.

Last, but certainly not least, was a fall that resulted in a very meaningful conversation with a neighbor. At this point, I was still able to walk without a walker, but my balance wasn't all that great. There were several little clean-up issues in the backyard (a few weeds in the lawn, a couple of rocks on the patio) that were bugging me. I had mentioned them to Barb, but it was obvious that the problem wasn't as significant in her view as it was in mine, because she had done nothing to address my issues. So, on a sunny morning, after she had headed out the door to run some errands, I headed out the door to rectify the problems myself. First on my agenda was the rock issue, so I staggered over to the spot where they had migrated out onto the patio. As I placed one foot on the rocks surrounding the patio, I immediately went down, falling amongst the plants. Of course, I attempted to get up without success, and after a short time, because it was rather warm lying there on the rocks, I decided to phone my neighbor. I knew that he was home, and he was always extremely helpful, so I knew that I could count on him to come to my rescue. Fortunately, I had remembered to take my phone with me; unfortunately, when I called, he didn't answer. I proceeded to leave a message, and hoped he would respond. He called me a few minutes later, explaining that he was on another call and apologizing for not responding immediately. He came by and extracted me from the landscaping. I thanked him for his help, he talked about how he felt that he was placed next door to be a help to me, and I told him that, just maybe, he was my neighbor so that I could be a help to him in some way. We proceeded to have a deeper conversation about life and faith. I really believe that God had other plans for my trip into the backyard and allowed me to fall so He could lift me up to be used for His purposes.

In addition to these examples of God's protection, I'm extremely thankful for His provision. He has met our every need from financial to physical. He has given us wonderful neighbors who have helped with all of the outdoor necessities from mowing the lawn to removing the snow. It's been extremely difficult for me to transition from being independent to a life of dependence; from relying on self to almost totally relying on others. They've watched, and graciously offered to help, as I attempted to do things myself because I thought that nobody could do them better. Then they waited until I was ready to reluctantly relinquish the ownership of my treasured activities to them. What I've been unable to do, they've done.

I'd guess that what I've shared with you may have confirmed what Barb has said all along and I think that I'm finally admitting to as well; that I was a stubborn, anal, secretive (at times—my add), German. Do you have any other names for me dear? Procrastinating? Now wait *just* a minute! Speaking of my wife—where do I start to recount the ways that God has blessed me through her life, aside from being a faithful wife and mother of my children? So much has changed for her as my disease has progressed, and she has sacrificed so much. She has been forced to do many of the things that she never did or were formerly her least favorite things to do. I did all of the driving when we traveled together; now *she* reluctantly does all of it. All of the things that I used to do, like outdoor work, heavy lifting, filling the car's gas tank, and other things, have all become part of her routine. She has had to help with virtually all of my personal care and accompanies me everywhere I need to go. Her dreams for our future have been drastically altered; dreams of having the freedom to go where we wanted when we wanted. My prayer for her is that one day she will be still be able to enjoy the things that she's sacrificed for me. As for my children, what a blessing it has been to have all of them offer to take us in and help with my care when it became too difficult for Barb.

Now for the answer to my final question: Will He rescue me from my presumed sure fate? The presumption here, since I have a disease for which there is currently no cure, is death. I guess that I could say that He's already done that, since I am assured of eternal life, but will I die? The Bible states that, …it is appointed unto men once to die…. (Hebrews 9:27a, KJV) So, what I'm really asking is, will this disease kill me? And the answer IS… I don't know. In the final analysis, the question is immaterial. Except for believers who will be alive when

Jesus returns, all of us will die of *some* cause. Through this disease, His *"painful mercy"* (Philippians 1:21, KJV) has made the Apostle Paul's statement, For to me to live is Christ, and to die is gain, real to me. "The threat of death has become a door to paradise." As I have gradually lost the ability to accomplish virtually anything on my own, I have gained the desire to live more completely for Him, and the things of heaven have become more desirable than the things of earth. This disease has truly been a blessing in disguise for me.

> **And we know that in all things God works for the good of those who love him, who have been called according to his purpose.**
> **—Romans 8:28, NIV**

Secret Sin \ Baermann

To God Be the Glory

My story of God's love and faithfulness continues. We now have ten grandchildren, with the anticipation of another by way of adoption. My son and his wife have blessed us with another grandson, evening the number of grandsons and granddaughters at five, and our oldest daughter and her husband are in the process of adopting a girl from Ethiopia. They've also volunteered to help Barb with my care by allowing us to live with them.

Today I'm sitting at my computer in the dining area of their (our) new residence in Central Wisconsin praising God for His goodness after experiencing His grace in miraculously providing everything we have needed over the past seven months. There are many details resulting from our move that still have to be resolved, but we have every confidence that God will be our help and strength through the remainder of the process.

Seven months ago, on a cold December day in northern Illinois, after months of living day-to-day in dealing with the progressive nature of my illness and my ability to climb the stairs in our two story home, and after experiencing a bout with sciatica in my right leg, we decided that we needed to start planning for the possibility of more difficult days ahead. We had already had several conversations with our kids about our future, so this was not a new discussion, and we reached a decision amazingly quickly about what we what we would do. So it was within a matter of days that we sat down with a realtor to begin the process of selling our home. Sales of homes had been extremely slow, so with the possibility of selling in a short time and for a reasonable price looking rather unlikely, we decided to put our home on the market after the first of the year praying that God would have His will and way in the process and would reveal to us how He wanted us to proceed.

Before the first of the year had a chance to arrive, my son-in-law, who lived down the street, approached me at the prompting of his parents who were visiting from out of town during the holidays with a story of diminished income due to a downturn in the economy that he anticipated would soon make it difficult to meet their mortgage payments. He had been contemplating short sale or foreclosure, and He wondered if something could be worked out to allow them to occupy our home and remain in the area so that their girls could remain in the same school district. After discussing the possibilities, we decided that, if they could get out from under their mortgage via short sale or foreclosure, they would rent our home by paying our mortgage costs and would purchase it from us at a later date when their credit status would allow them to obtain another mortgage. This would not only decrease their costs for housing in the short run, but would allow them to escape an upside down position on their current mortgage and convert it to a right side up position in the future. So instead of our house needing to be sold, God would now have to provide a way to make all of that happen.

Now all that was needed would be to actually see that accomplished, find a buyer for my daughter and son-in-law's house in Wisconsin, and find another home to purchase that would meet all of our needs up there. All of this needed to happen within a time-frame that would meet my need for care, and all in an extremely slow market. Chances of all of these things happening smoothly seemed to be slim to none but it wouldn't be too difficult at all for a God who loves us, can do all things, and holds our future in His hands.

He began His work as we watched and marveled. Our daughter and her husband in Illinois got a short sale offer rather quickly on their home. Of course, the long, tedious process of bank approval still was ahead with all of the questions that would accompany it, but nevertheless, it was an offer. My daughter and her husband in Wisconsin approached some friends in their town who had been attempting to sell one of two homes that they owned in the area, the one in town being perfect for our needs, and they agreed to allow them (us) to purchase it (with our help) if my daughter could sell her home. So she listed their home on a "by owner" website, and after what seemed as though forever but was really only a short time all things considered, and only two responses, they received the offer that they had hoped for.

I have left out so many of the details of our family's journey and the feelings that accompanied the process; details that involved not only the scope of all that needed to happen, but the timing of it all, and feelings that sometimes included anxiousness, doubt and (dare I say) unbelief at times. But God was never overwhelmed by the circumstances, and despite our trepidation, was always in control of every aspect of our journey. He was showing Himself to be mighty to handle every situation and blessing us at every turn, all the while testing and growing our faith in Him.

I guess that what I'm saying again is, GOD IS GOOD, ALL THE TIME, and HE LOVES YOU! He can and will be in control of every aspect of your journey through life if you will allow Him to be, and His desire is to bless you in ways that you won't believe. I don't know why (except for God bringing it to mind), but suddenly I'm thinking of this old hymn, "Trust and Obey" (I recommend that you go to this website and read and listen www.hymns.me.uk/trust-and-obey-favorite-hymn.htm). I know that the popularity of hymns has waned over the years, but the truth of this hymn endures and so does the reality of the fact that our lives could be so rewarding if we'd just trust and obey the Savior who loves us and wants what's best for us.

> **Now to him who is able to do immeasurably more than all we ask or imagine, according to his power that is at work within us, to him be glory in the church and in Christ Jesus throughout all generations, forever and ever! Amen.**
>
> **—Ephesians 3:20-21, NIV**

Secret Sin \ Baermann

Conclusion

A QUESTION that I was told that I should know the answer to was, "Who do you want your readership to be?" Should it be for Christians or non-Christians? So I asked myself the question, Why wouldn't someone like me, someone who has never written a book, is not looking to make a career of it, and who probably won't write another one want everyone to read it? Besides, isn't after you've written the book the *wrong* time to be asking that question? Well, because I respect the person who suggested it, I did. The answer that I came up with was... everyone.

Everyone needs to read this book whether they think they need to or not. If not, it would be like saying some people don't need the Gospel, or some people don't need Jesus. I hope that doesn't sound arrogant to you. Maybe it would be better to limit it to those who *think* that they need Jesus, or are at the very least considering their need of Him. They have grasped a portion of the truth. They, like me, have been deceived in some way, either by the lies of the evil one or by their own ignorance. Now that you've finished it, I'd encourage you to give this book to someone who you know is struggling and can't seem to find the answer to their problem. They don't have to be enslaved to the same sin that I was; but they have to know HIM if they are to gain the victory over their sin.

Remember that there is a more blessed way.

Trusting > Believing
Repenting > Confessing

SANCTIFICATION > SALVATION
SALVATION = Confessing + Believing
SANCTIFICATION = Repenting + Trusting

All who have been saved by God's marvelous grace are on a journey between *Salvation* and *Sanctification*. It takes a whole lifetime to complete the trip. Some are not on this journey yet. They're headed in the other direction. Those of us who are may have left *Salvation* without any written directions to *Sanctification*. Others may have packed a map; still others may be fortunate enough to have a GPS. Some may be in the midst of their trip, but now find themselves sitting beside the road either broken down or out of gas (because they didn't change the oil or have the gas gage fixed when they noticed it was broken). Some could have taken a detour or seem to be temporarily lost and are frantically searching for their maps or have pulled over to ask for directions. Some have stopped at every attraction along the way that looked interesting. Others are sailing along with their GPS set and recalculating their route, radio on and top down on their convertibles. When all of us finally reach the end of our trip, we'll arrive with vehicles that reflect our journeys; with dents that tell of our driving habits and engines that are sputtering or running smoothly based on the maintenance that's been performed. The good news is…we get the new model when we arrive that's designed to be maintenance free.

My point is that we will get there, but we have a lot to do during the process and there are all sorts of decisions to be made along the way. The Holy Spirit is our helper, but he will not help without our cooperation. In that sense:

Salvation is God's gift to us—
Sanctification is our gift to Him.

Salvation (as great a gift as it is) is little more than agreeing with God. *Sanctification* is showing the world who HE is and that what HE says is true. Give Him the gift of yourself. Don't thank Him by giving Him less.

Conclusion

I appeal to you therefore, brothers, by the mercies of God, to present your bodies as a living sacrifice, holy and acceptable to God, which is your spiritual worship. Do not be conformed to this world, but be transformed by the renewal of your mind, that by testing you may discern what is the will of God, what is good and acceptable and perfect.

—Romans 12:1-2, ESV

TO BE CONTINUED

Growing Your Faith One Page at a Time

Resources for Adult Bible Studies, Sunday School, Individual Studies

GraceAcresPress.com

www.ingramcontent.com/pod-product-compliance
Lightning Source LLC
Chambersburg PA
CBHW052113070526
44584CB00017B/2467